J. M. BARRIE

J. M. BARRIE

J. M. Barrie

A WALCK MONOGRAPH

by

Roger Lancelyn Green

HENRY Z. WALCK, INCORPORATED

NEW YORK

CONTENTS

To
Three Pirates
PETER COTES
LIONEL GADSDEN
WILLIAM LUFF
(Starkey, Captain Hook, Cecco)
whose friendship I owe
to
PETER PAN

A Note About the Author

A house full of books took the place of a more formal education for Roger Lancelyn Green until he went to Oxford, and interested him in those branches of literature and legend which he has made his particular study.

After taking his B.Litt., for which he presented a thesis on Andrew Lang, he was for a year a professional actor, one part he played being that of the pirate Noodler in *'Peter Pan'*—which led to the writing of *Fifty Years of Peter Pan*. He was also an antiquarian bookseller and Deputy Librarian at Merton College, Oxford, before settling at Poulton-Lancelyn, the manor house where his ancestors have lived for nine hundred years. Since then he has written several adventure stories for children, some of them set against a background of Greek mythology. However, his interest in legend is not confined to Greece, and he has retold *King Arthur and his Knights of the Round Table*, *Robin Hood* and *The Saga of Asgard*.

While holding a Fellowship in English Literature at Liverpool University Roger Lancelyn Green edited *The Diaries of Lewis Carroll*, having already written *The Story of Lewis Carroll* for children and *Tellers of Tales* and other works on famous writers for children—amongst whom Barrie, Carroll, Lang and Mrs Molesworth have been favourites for many years.

1. Windows in Thrums

'To be born is to be wrecked on an island.' James Matthew Barrie was cast ashore on May 9th, 1860, in a four-room cottage in the Brechin Road of the little town of Kirriemuir, seventeen miles north of Dundee, surrounded by some of the most beautiful country in Scotland. He was the third son and ninth child (but two daughters had died in infancy) of a handloom weaver, David Barrie, and his wife Margaret Ogilvy—so called, after the Scottish custom, by her family and friends even after her marriage. One more daughter, Maggie, was born three years later; but Alexander, the eldest of the family, was already at Aberdeen University in 1860, where he prospered so well that he soon became a master at Glasgow Academy, and before long one of the first of Her Majesty's Inspectors of Schools.

The Barrie household was typical of the God-fearing, industrious and ambitious Scots of the last two centuries, living in the strange combination of almost savage independence and a truly Christian sense of communal duty and fellowship so well depicted by Barrie in his later 'Thrums' novels. The driving ambition and enthusiasm for learning, which called out the utmost of application and self-denial in the family, would have sent all three of the Barrie sons to the University, though David and his wife and daughters had gone hungry to do so. Alec had already proved that such sacrifices were not made in vain, and David the second son showed every sign of succeeding as triumphantly in his bid for the Ministry, had he not slipped on the ice just before his fourteenth birthday, fractured his skull and died within the day.

Jamie Barrie was six at the time, and the tragic death of his mother's best loved son with all that it entailed was the most profound and far-reaching influence on his whole life and character of any that came to him in his childhood. Yet the influence could only have had its amazing effect on the child who was already endowed with the strange streak of genius that made him J. M. Barrie.

In *Margaret Ogilvy*, one of the most moving and revealing books ever written—and to many unreadably, even revoltingly so—Barrie tells of his mother's grief and prostration, of its shattering impact on himself, and of how he set about taking David's place and dedicating himself to bringing back her smile and to winning fame and fortune so that every joy and comfort could be heaped upon her. The initial determination and the plan for the golden future is common to many a small boy, even without the tragic incentive of a brother's death: the uncanny thing in Barrie's case is not so much the achievement in every detail—though this would seem wildly improbable were it fiction and not fact—as the unimaginable corollary that to do so he must remain in many essentials a child until it was done.

To read *Margaret Ogilvy* is to wonder also whether Barrie's mother did not remain to some extent a child also; but this is unsafe to assume, since we can now see her only through the magic glass of her son's description. And his curse throughout life, which was also the gift of genius which made him what he was, like that of his own *Sentimental Tommy*, was the over-vivid imagination which could so colour what he saw or felt or remembered, that the perfect picture became in the end indistinguishable to his mind from the truth: 'It's easy for you that has just one mind; but if you had as many minds as I have!' as he was to make Tommy cry in desperation.

Childhood was not all overshadowed by his self-imposed task of comforting Margaret Ogilvy, and Barrie enjoyed to the full the delights shared by his Kirriemuir contemporaries. In fact, when he was playing, he played more fully, we may assume, than any of them, entering into their games with the absorption and self-abandon which makes them so nearly real to the imaginative child.

To begin with there were the ordinary pranks that have been common from time immemorial. Barrie's friend of those days, James Robb (who later lent his name to a minor pirate in *Peter Pan*), remembered nearly seventy years later how they played at 'chickie mailie', as described in *Sentimental Tommy*:

'Into the woodwork of the east window they had thrust a pin, to which a button was tied, and the button was also attached to a long string. They hunkered afar off and pulled this string, and then the button tapped the death-rap on the window, and the sport was successful, for [the occupant] screamed.'

Or again, how they tricked one of the bailies of Kirriemuir who found a parcel lying in the middle of the Brechin Road, picked it up and proceeded with it under his arm—whence it was jerked suddenly and mysteriously by a long, unseen string, the other end of which was in Barrie's hand.

Among more lawful sports his favourite was already cricket, played at Kirriemuir with a home-made bat and a flat boulder set on end for a wicket. He developed the amazing straightness of eye and dexterity of hand which continued to astonish his friends throughout his life. He was, moreover, practically ambidextrous, being born left-handed but taught to use his right: long after, when suffering from acute scrivener's cramp, he began writing with his left hand which he soon learnt to do far more neatly than with his right. Being Barrie, he decided that he thought down his left arm in a more sinister vein than his right, and pointed to his later works, such as *Mary Rose* and *Farewell, Miss Julie Logan*, as a proof of this.

Neither chickie mailie nor cricket—nor the more mysterious games he mentions, such as peeries, preens, pilly and palaulays—were the most absorbing of the boy Jamie's occupations, however. His vivid imagination and the disconcerting power of mental shape-shifting found vent in make-believe of various kinds. Kirriemuir had a fine tradition of loyalty to 'the King over the water', and very soon Barrie was leading the last Jacobite rebellion, and was himself Prince Charlie hiding in a 'lair' above the little stream which flowed through the valley on the outskirts of the town, known as 'the Den'. The whole new page in Jacobite history is graphically described in *Sentimental Tommy*, and doubtless Barrie's imagination painted the scene so vividly that we might almost take as autobiographical Tommy's sentimental picture in *Tommy and Grizel* of Corp Shiach's vain search for 'the Den' to show to his own small son in after life:

'He set out blithely, but to his bewilderment he could not find the lair. It had not been a tiny hollow where muddy water gathered; he remembered an impregnable fortress full of men whose armour rattled as they came and went, so this could not be the lair. He had taken the wrong way to it, for the way was across a lagoon, up a deep-flowing river, then by horse till the rocky ledge terrified all four-footed things; no, up a grassy slope had never been the way . . .'

Other games took place in the little square washing-house (eight feet by six) behind his home in the Brechin Road. These included dramatic adventures in which the final 'act' consisted of trying to put each other into the copper. In the Dedication to *Peter Pan* he wrote:

'This washing-house is not only the theatre of my first play, but has a still closer connection with Peter. It is the original of the little house the Lost Boys built in the Never, Never Land for Wendy, and the chief difference is that it never wore John's tall hat as a chimney. If Robb had owned a lum hat I have no doubt that it would have been placed on the washing-house.'

Most of these games of the imagination demanded some sort of background of a literary nature, and, as would be expected, Barrie was an early and an avid reader. Less expectedly, perhaps, others of the household read much and widely, beyond the usual careful and continual study of the Bible. His mother, Barrie tells us, was as keen a bookworm as he himself, and she 'with ten minutes to spare before the starch was ready would begin the *Decline and Fall*—and finish it, too, that winter'. They would read books together— '*Robinson Crusoe* being the first (and the second)'—and soon Barrie was deep in as many as he could lay hands on. He tells us:

'*The Pilgrim's Progress* we had in the house, and so enamoured of it was I that I turned our garden into Sloughs of Despond, with peasticks to represent Christian on his travels and a buffet-stool for his burden. . . . Besides reading every book we could hire or borrow I also bought one now and again, and while buying (it was the occupation of weeks) I read, standing at the counter, most of the other books in the shop, which is perhaps the most exquisite way of reading. And I took in a magazine called *Sunshine*, the most delicious periodical, I am sure, of any day. It cost a halfpenny or a penny a month, and always, as I fondly remember, had a continued tale about the dearest girl, who sold water-cress, which is a dainty not grown, and I suppose never seen in my native town. . . . I know not whether it was owing to her loitering on the way one month to an extent flesh and blood could not bear, or because we had exhausted the penny library, but one day I conceived a glorious idea: why should I not write the tales myself? I did write them—in the garret. . . . They were all tales of adventure (happiest is he who writes of adventure), no

14

characters were allowed within it if I knew their like in the flesh, the scene lay in unknown parts, desert islands, enchanted gardens, with knights on black chargers, and round the first corner a lady selling water-cress.'

By the time he began writing stories Barrie had begun his formal education, though he learnt to read and write at home. At the age of six he was attending the little mixed school kept by the two Misses Adam whose father, a retired clergyman, had come to live in Kirriemuir. This was the basis of 'the Hanky School, which was for the genteel and for the common who contemplated soaring' described in *Sentimental Tommy* and, at one further remove, of the school kept by the Misses Throssel in *Quality Street*.

After a year there, however, Barrie was removed to the Free Church School to be drilled in the rudiments of classical learning before proceeding to Glasgow Academy where his brother Alec, who was now a master, had offered to superintend his education and house him during term time. He remained there for three years, returning when his brother left the Academy, though not to Kirriemuir, since his parents moved in 1871 to Forfar, five miles away. Steam had come to Kirriemuir, and the old handloom weavers were fast going out of work: 'Before I reached my tenth year a giant entered my native place in the night and we woke to find him in possession,' wrote Barrie. 'Where had formerly been but the click of the shuttle was soon the roar of "power", handlooms were pushed into a corner.' David Barrie, though he was fifty-five by now, uprooted

15

himself at the right moment and obtained a job in the counting-house of a linen factory.

But he was away for less than two years, for in 1872 he returned to Kirriemuir, having done so well that he was made principal clerk at another new factory which was about to open there. This was a distinct step up, both as to position and income, and the Barries, instead of returning to 'The Tenements' in the Brechin Road, were able to buy 'Strath View' at the junction of the Glamis and Forfar roads: a strange, many-cornered house with a big window set in the angle with a view of both roads, and also down into Kirriemuir—the original 'Window in Thrums'.

After a few terms at Forfar, Barrie returned to the Kirriemuir school until he was thirteen, when his brother, now an Inspector of Schools for the Dumfries district in south-west Scotland, once again took charge of him for five years of uninterrupted education at Dumfries Academy, broken only by short holidays at 'Strath View'.

These years at Dumfries Barrie described afterwards as the happiest of his life. He worked hard, won prizes and enjoyed learning; he was good enough at organised games to pass muster with the more athletic boys; he could fight if necessary, but was more apt at making friends, with whom he went for long walks, visiting likely burns and lochs for trout-fishing, and ruined castles such as Torthowald and Thrieve for their romantic interest.

He read more and more widely (one of his school-friends was the son of the local bookseller, who gave him the run of the shop), revelling in the pirates and redskins of Ballantyne, Kingston and Ascott Hope, finding 'wrecked islands' in their pages and in those of Marryat and Jules Verne, secret codes in Edgar Allan Poe, more of the Wild West in Fenimore Cooper, before passing on by way of Dickens and Thackeray to the flaming style of the local 'great man', Thomas Carlyle (then living near Dumfries), whom he would waylay in an ecstasy of hero-worship, and then not dare to address.

In the earlier years at Dumfries the old games of the Kirriemuir 'Den' variety were revived and carried to thrilling extremes, usually in company with Hal and Stuart Gordon, sons of the Sheriff Clerk, in their pleasant and extensive garden at 'Moat Brae'. 'When the shades of night began to fall,' he and his friends, Barrie told a younger generation in a speech delivered at a Dumfries Academy prize-giving in 1924,

'. . . crept up walls and down trees and became pirates in a sort of Odyssey that was long afterwards to become the play of *Peter Pan*. For our escapades in a certain Dumfries garden, which is enchanted land to me, were certainly the genesis of that nefarious work.'

And as early as 1913 he had written in his Preface to a new edition of *The Coral Island*:

'It egged me on, not merely to be wrecked every Saturday for many months in a long-suffering garden, but to my first work of fiction, a record of our adventures, *The Log-Book*. We had a sufficiently mysterious cave, that had not been a cave until we named it, and here we grimly ate coconuts, stoned from the trees which not even Jack nor Ralph nor Peterkin would have recognised as likely to bear them.'

More important still was an awakening of interest in the drama and the writing of his first play. There was a theatre in Dumfries, very small, but visited by London stars from time to time—including J. L. Toole and George Shelton, who were afterwards to act in several of his plays. The little Dumfries theatre was, Barrie tells us:

'. . . the first I ever entered; so it was the one I liked best. I entered many times in my schooldays. . . . I had the good fortune to frequent it in what was one of its great years [1876-7]. . . . It was in those schooldays that I had an experience not always vouchsafed to greater mortals —I went 'behind the scenes'. . . . Such doings led inevitably to the forming of a dramatic club at school for which I wrote my first play, *Bandelero the Bandit*.'

This was performed that same winter, accompanied by two other plays 'based' on two favourites from Toole's repertoire: for, as no copies were available, the company re-wrote them from memory. Barrie played the heroine in the 'vamped' version of John Poole's *Paul Pry*, on condition he played the hero in C. Scott's *Off the Line*. *Bandelero* came last—'a melodrama in six scenes and fifteen minutes, in which I played all my favourite characters in fiction, artfully rolled into one'.

But this was almost the last of the amateur theatricals. In 1878 Barrie was eighteen, and having completed his education at Dumfries but failed to obtain a scholarship, he proceeded to Edinburgh University, still financed by his devoted elder brother. The desire to write was now strong upon him, still coupled with his devotion to the theatre, and his brother seems to have had this in mind when Edinburgh was chosen, for there he came under David Masson, one of the leading professors of Literature of the day: a great teacher, a fine scholar and an accomplished man of letters.

Barrie was already determined that Literature was to be his profession, once he had taken his degree, in which it was only one of a variety of subjects. First, however, he must give almost his whole time to study for that degree to become a Master of Arts, and not let down those who had struggled to get him into a university at all. So for four years it was mainly, as he wrote in *Vagabond Students*:

> 'Grind, grind, grind,
> With eyelids heavy and red;
> A student sat in his lonely digs
> With a wet towel round his head.'

But writing was not altogether banished. Indeed, Barrie became a part-time professional journalist while still at the University, reviewing books and plays for *The Edinburgh Courant*, and even an occasional concert for *The Dumfries Herald*—though he was utterly unmusical. 'I can never tell one tune from another. I dislike music,' he confessed later to Rosaline Masson, the Professor's younger daughter, adding wryly, 'I was musical critic for several years!'

As the constant visits to theatres in his capacity of dramatic critic resulted in meeting several actors and managers, Barrie attempted another play, called *Bohemia* (with a scene set, of all unlikely places, in 'a glade in Brighton'). But none of his theatrical acquaintances showed any interest in it; the manuscript was flung aside, and he resumed his more serious studies.

He took his M.A. in April 1882, just before his twenty-second birthday, and after a summer in Kirriemuir returned to Edinburgh to combine desultory reviewing for the *Courant* with researches for a learned work on English Literature, which he felt that he must produce to prove that he was right in following his literary ambitions rather than reading Law.

But nothing came of it, and he returned to Kirriemuir at Christmas, anxious and dispirited, not knowing what to do—except that he was determined to be an author. Then his sister Jane Annie chanced to see an advertisement for a 'leader-writer' for *The Nottingham Journal*. Barrie applied in desperation (with a testimonial from Masson)—and was offered the post, at three pounds a week.

II. An Admirable Crichton

'What makes you write, Mr Barrie?' asked one of the child actresses during the first rehearsals of *Peter Pan*. 'Why, don't you know, Nibs?' he answered. 'My fingers are full of ink, and it *must* come out.'

The ink was needed as soon as Barrie arrived in Nottingham at the end of January 1883, with his first 'leader' scribbled on the end-papers of a copy of Horace during the journey. Five leaders a week were expected (average length twelve hundred words); but as if this was not enough, he was soon contributing book reviews, and then literary columns on Mondays and Thursdays. In addition to this a serial story called *Vagabond Students* in eleven parts appeared in the weekly supplement between June and August of that year; and his one-act farce, *Caught Napping: A Comedietta*, after occupying most of a page in the *Journal* on May 30th, 1883, was reprinted in a little pamphlet—now the rarest of all Barrie's published works.

The play reflected Barrie's continuing interest in the theatre, and was written for the actress Minnie Palmer, who was playing in Nottingham and whom Barrie worshipped from afar. He seems actually to have met her and given her a copy of the play, but it was never acted and soon forgotten. Barrie continued to be susceptible to female charms, and worshipped quite a number of actresses in this way; but in their company he was overcome with shyness and could hardly utter a word. He was extremely self-conscious at this time, partly on account of his smallness (he was five foot one, and very slightly built), and was convinced of his insignificance to the female eye. 'The saddest words a broken-hearted young man can have applied to him' by a woman, he wrote in an anonymous article in 1887, 'is that he is "quite harmless".' Nevertheless, like the young journalist in *Caught Napping*, he could make 'a blush on a woman's face supply material for a half column paragraph', and many another subject too, as his prodigious industry grew and broadened.

There were no more plays and stories in *The Nottingham Journal* in 1884, but articles began to find their way into London periodicals towards the end of the year, so that he was not left quite destitute when his appointment finished suddenly at the end of October because the proprietors decided to substitute syndicated articles and dispense with their own leader-writer.

Barrie returned to Kirriemuir, and bombarded the London editors with long-distance articles. Frederick Greenwood of *The St James's Gazette*, in returning one, scribbled on it, 'But I liked that Scotch thing. Any more of those?' This had been 'An Auld Licht Community' which he published on November 17th, 1884, and Barrie at once set to work on 'An Auld Licht Funeral', which appeared on January 9th, 1885, and was followed by six others in the *St James's*, and as many in *Home Chimes* later that year.

Though Greenwood could give him no permanent commission, Barrie came to London at the end of March 1885, took a room near the British Museum, and flung himself into free-lance journalism with even more amazing industry than he had shown at Nottingham.

The struggle was hard at first, and he may even have gone hungry on occasion; but within five years he was not only able to let journalism sink quietly into the background, but was hailed as one of the coming authors of the day.

Barrie's first book, the short topical skit *Better Dead*, appeared in November 1887 and he had still to pay for its publication. But W. Robertson Nicoll, editor of *The British Weekly*, for whom he was now writing the serial story afterwards published as *When a Man's Single*, suggested that he should collect and revise his sketches of the Auld Lichts, and was able to secure their publication in 1888 as *Auld Licht Idylls*.

With this book Barrie achieved immediate fame, increased by *When a Man's Single* at the end of the year. Positive celebrity followed when *A Window in Thrums*, a further collection of Auld Licht stories, appeared in the following July, and was confirmed when his Thrums novel, *The Little Minister*, was published in 1891.

Although Thrums is an almost accurate picture of Kirriemuir, the period of Barrie's stories and sketches is seldom that of his own youth. When as a small boy he first began his self-imposed task of comforting his mother and bringing back the smile which had fled at David's death, a ready way of achieving this was to lure her into telling stories of her own childhood. In *Margaret Ogilvy* he confesses:

'The reason my books deal with the past instead of with the life I myself have known is simply this, that I soon grow tired of writing tales unless I can see a little girl, of whom my mother has told me, wandering confidently through the pages. Such a grip has her memory of her girlhood had upon me since I was a boy of six. . . .

'She was eight when her mother's death made her mistress of the house and mother to her little brother. . . . She told me everything, and so my memories of our little red town are coloured by her memories. I knew it as it had been for generations, and suddenly I saw it change, and the transformation could not fail to strike a boy, for these first years are the most impressionable (nothing that happens after we are twelve matters very much); they are also the most vivid years when we look back. . . . The new town is to me a glass through which I look at the old, the people I see passing up and down these wynds are less those I saw in my childhood than their fathers and mothers who did these things in the same way when my mother was young.'

The essential truth of Barrie's picture of Thrums is vouched for by Alexander Whyte (1836-1921), famous in his day as a preacher in Edinburgh, who was born at Kirriemuir of humbler parentage than Barrie himself:

'Mr. Barrie has thoroughly grasped the characters of the little community, with all their humour and pathos. *Thrums* is a true picture of my native place.'

Margaret Ogilvy, who was also responsible for so much of the dialect, which was already dying out when Barrie was a boy, was herself brought up as a member of the Auld Licht Community (Barrie was a Free Churchman), her father being one of the leading followers of the 'Old Light' in Kirriemuir. The sect believed in a return to the early Church as described in the New Testament; their church was little more than a barn; music, hymns and written sermons were forbidden, and they chose their own ministers: the Auld Licht character 'was austere and fervent, but it lacked the graces'. An exact contemporary of Barrie's, whom I met nearly twenty years ago while I was touring Scotland in *Peter Pan*, remembered the Auld Lichts well and assured me that Barrie had by no means over-drawn them.

A Window in Thrums was more skilfully written than *Auld Licht Idylls*, but once again used separate sketches and did not make the rounded whole demanded of a novel—any more than did the picturesque romance of *When a Man's Single*, which Barrie wrote one chapter ahead of the serial publication and based largely on his experiences as a journalist in Nottingham. But with *The Little Minister* he tried seriously to write a novel, set in Thrums in the early nineteenth century, and almost succeeded. Its great charm lies, as with all Barrie's works, in the style and characterisation; the slight and rather improbable plot cannot and should not try to stand alone. It turns on the young Auld Licht minister, Gavin Dishart, who falls in love with Babbie the gipsy, marries her 'over the tongs' in Romany style, and is besieged in his manse by the shocked elders of his congregation. All ends happily, however, when he shows his worth by rescuing one of them from a flooded river, and Babbie turns out to be the ward of the local laird, Lord Rintoul, from whom she has run away.

Meanwhile Barrie was toying once again with his

25

second love, the theatre, and with more chance of success this time, though by no means at the first attempt. His dramatic career in London began with a play which his friend Marriott Watson planned to write about the eighteenth-century poet, Richard Savage. He asked his friend's help, and Barrie seems not to have done a great deal more than rewrite from Watson's script. *Richard Savage* was given a single matinée performance on April 16th, 1891, without exciting any interest or finding a manager to give it a full production.

The next attempt, however, was much more successful, and opened on May 30th of the same year. It was a one-act play this time, by Barrie alone, a burlesque called *Ibsen's Ghost*, which J. L. Toole put on and acted in, supported by George Shelton and Irene Vanbrugh. This riotously funny sequel to *Hedda Gabler*, with topical references to other controversial plays which were on at the time, such as *A Doll's House* and Michel Carré's mime *L'Enfant Prodigue*, made Toole eager for a full-length play by this new dramatist. Knowing so well what Toole's admirers would expect, Barrie constructed a slight but most entertaining farce called *Walker, London* ('Walker!' was a catchword at the time for accusing someone of pulling one's leg) about a barber who runs away on his wedding day to have the honeymoon by himself and, masquerading as a famous African explorer, is welcomed by a party of young people spending a holiday in a houseboat on the Thames. After many amusing situations he escapes, undetected until he is actually leaving, when they shout

26

after him for his address, and he replies, 'Walker, London!' which they repeat, realising they have been hoaxed, as the curtain falls.

Although the play ran for 511 performances, Barrie got little from it but prestige value, as he had sold it outright to Toole. But he set to work at once on another play, this time for Sir Henry Irving, who had advised Toole to take both *Ibsen's Ghost* and *Walker, London*, and wrote *The Professor's Love Story*—a slight, preposterous and rather sentimental comedy, but of great and enduring charm; the first real example of the unique blend of humour, sentiment and whimsicality, overlaying an unexpectedly deep and universal problem, which constitutes the more tangible aspects of Barrie's genius.

In this case the depths were but slight, and Irving considered the play too airy a bubble for the great traditions of the Lyceum. Toole, Alexander and Hare followed suit, but on Irving's recommendation the actor-manager E. S. Willard bought the American rights and put it on in New York on December 19th, 1892, with great success. It did not reach London for two years, but when Willard finally presented it there in June 1894, it ran for nearly six months, and has twice been revived since then. It is not a play in which the plot is important or can be epitomised, dealing simply with the charmingly absent-minded and unworldly Professor Goodwillie, who falls in love with his secretary without realising what the symptoms mean, runs away to Thrums from the titled lady who wants to marry him and is caught up in a merry and bucolic harvesting in

27

which the proper couples are happily sorted out in time for the final curtain.

A great advance on this was the dramatic version of *The Little Minister*, in which plot and character are nicely balanced, with humour and charm to set off the pleasant 'period romance' of the whole. The action takes place in Thrums at the time of the Weavers' Riots (put back a few years to 1840) and the plot is far better constructed than that of the novel.

Once again, as with all Barrie's plays, a synopsis could do little justice to the literary and dramatic quality of the whole, which is a delight to read and absolute magic on the stage. This was Barrie's first really outstanding success both in England and America, and made over £80,000 in its first ten years. It ran for 320 performances (opening on November 6th, 1897) at the Haymarket, with Cyril Maude as Gavin, and was revived several times, besides touring widely. It was immensely popular and well loved: 'a beautiful play, beautifully acted,' wrote Lewis Carroll in his diary a few weeks before his death, '*The Little Minister* is a play I should like to see again and again.'

Meanwhile, in 1894, Barrie had married Mary Ansell, the actress who played one of the girls in *Walker, London*, and settled in Gloucester Road, South Kensington—accompanied by the huge St Bernard dog, Porthos. Besides a one-act adaptation of some scenes from *Vanity Fair*, his only other dramatic venture, in 1893, had been the libretto of a comic opera in which Conan Doyle assisted with many of the lyrics. In the printed version Barrie added humorous marginalia supposed to be written by one of the characters, a small page-boy called Caddy. The opera was not a success, but Barrie was sufficiently philosophic about it to write for Doyle a clever little parody of a Sherlock Holmes story, called *The Adventure of the Two Collaborators*.

Doyle was a close friend at this time, and an early member of Barrie's team of amateur cricketers, the 'Allahakbarries', who played an occasional match against village elevens, and a regular one for many years running against a team of artists at Broadway in Gloucestershire. The name originated in the train on the way to the first match, when Barrie found it necessary to instruct more than one of his players 'in the finesse of the game: which was the side of the bat you hit with, for instance'. Two of the team were African explorers, and Barrie asked Joseph Thomson what was the Arabic for 'Heaven help us'. The answer being 'Allah akbar', a title for the team was found without difficulty. Doyle was the only really good player in the Allahakbarries, though A. E. W. Mason proved himself a good fast bowler; but of the rest Barrie wrote that 'the more distinguished as authors his men were the worse they played,' and described how 'Maurice Hewlett could sometimes look well set just before he came out,' or 'Charles Whibley threw in unerringly but in the wrong direction.'

Before the success of his plays turned him wholly to the theatre, Barrie continued to write novels; and indeed some critics regretted that he ever succumbed to the glamour of the stage which, as Doyle for example held, 'diverted from literature the man with the purest style of his age'. The novels did not come very easily, however, and after *The Little Minister* it was nearly five years before the next was ready, and even then it had run away with Barrie to such an extent that he had to issue the story of his hero's boyhood as *Sentimental Tommy* in 1896 and keep the rest of his scheme for a sequel.

It was a long, strange book with very little shape, telling how Tommy Sandys began his life in a London slum, and, on his mother's death, was brought to Thrums with his baby sister Elspeth. Tommy's boyhood is studied in detail, with entrancing descriptions of the imaginative games which he organised with Elspeth, his faithful friend Corp and the lonely little girl Grizel, daughter of another outcast, the 'Painted Lady'. But the underlying study is of Tommy's character—which might under less happy circumstances have been that of Barrie himself, who could see so clearly the dangers besetting the dreamer, the escapist and the creative artist blessed —or cursed—with the imaginative temperament which was his own penalty of genius. 'He had a devouring desire to try on other folks' feelings, as if they were so many suits of clothes,' says the schoolmaster of Tommy.

Despite the boyish delight in all Tommy's youthful ploys and imaginings, there was a slight undertone of bitterness which surprised readers who expected the frank romanticism of *The Little Minister*. But when the sequel, *Tommy and Grizel*, appeared in 1900 the escapists received a very rude shock indeed: for the book is stark tragedy and almost brutally merciless as it probes into Tommy's failure to grow up and come to grips with adult life, to face reality squarely instead of

30

shying off into the imagined situations in which such as Tommy hide from the world.

'Poor Tommy! he was still a boy, he was ever a boy, trying sometimes, as now, to be a man, and always when he looked round he ran back to his boyhood as if he saw it holding out its arms to him and inviting him to come back and play. He was so fond of being a boy that he could not grow up.'

In spite of its obvious relation to *Peter Pan*, *Tommy and Grizel* must not be taken as autobiographical, except to the extent that Barrie was the kind of man who could experience enough of Tommy's particular tragedy to understand it and follow it to the conclusions which he himself never approached. Like Tommy, he might have said of it:

'I had no say in the matter; the thing demanded of me that I should do it and I had to do it.'

The urge which produced *Tommy and Grizel* led Barrie in 1900 to write his only problem play, *The Wedding Guest*, though plays of the kind were popular at the time, the influence of Ibsen having affected even such dramatists as Wilde and Pinero, while laying the foundations for the theatre of Shaw and Galsworthy.

'Ibsen? Queer now to think that Ibsen was once considered advanced!' says the New Man in Barrie's one-act skit, *Punch*, produced in 1906. Barrie's problem play of the mistress (plus baby) who turns up at her ex-lover's wedding, and then denounces him to the

31

over-sheltered bride, is good strong stuff of the kind then demanded, but was either too 'advanced' or not convincingly worked out: it ran for only a hundred performances and has not been revived.

Then, wisely, he turned back to the romance and charm which had captivated so many audiences in *The Little Minister* and wrote *Quality Street*—as fragile as egg-shell china and as delicate. Set in the Napoleonic period with a background that recalls *Cranford*, it is an artificial comedy of great theatrical skill, and yet real and poignant even in this very different age. For Phoebe's problem when 'the gallant Captain Brown' returns after ten years to find her so changed and aged, is a real and universal one, in spite of the setting; and her instinctive solution of it is perfectly true to life— even if in life such situations do not often reach so happy an outcome.

Quality Street is still one of Barrie's most popular plays, both on the professional and amateur stages. In the published version, with his amusing stage directions, it reads as a pleasant, rather romantic 'period' story, and is a particular favourite with younger readers—girls, perhaps, rather than boys.

The next play, one of Barrie's most completely successful and one of the two or three which give him an assured place among our greater dramatists, was *The Admirable Crichton*, also produced in 1902, about six weeks after *Quality Street*. The basic idea came from a suggestion made by Conan Doyle while staying with Barrie at Kirriemuir in 1893: 'If a king and an able seaman were wrecked together on a desert island for the rest of their lives, the sailor would end as king and the monarch as his servant.' From this grew Barrie's parable of the Earl of Loam and his party, cast away on their island and helpless in this new setting until Crichton the butler, who in the first act has been the perfect servant in an aristocratic household, takes control and shows himself to be the natural master in the given circumstances. By the end of the third act the situation is approaching its remorsely logical conclusion, with Crichton as undisputed king about to choose the Earl's eldest daughter as his bride, when the rescue party reaches the island—summoned by Crichton who fires the beacon at the supreme moment, though he knows what the result will be. In the last act Crichton is once more the butler in Lord Loam's Mayfair house, while all the party have slipped back into their original characters, and their reactions to the island adventure point the moral and underline the quiet satire on the values of civilisation.

'It deals,' remarked the old actor Sir Squire Bancroft in melancholy tones to A. E. W. Mason after the first night, 'with the juxtaposition of the drawing-room and the servants' hall—always to me a very painful subject.'

III. The Boy Who Wouldn't Grow Up

All Barrie's life led up to the creation of Peter Pan, and everything that he had written so far contained hints or foreshadowings of what was to come. Sentimental Tommy himself had devised the first draft for the story:

'It was but a reverie about a little boy who was lost. His parents find him in a wood singing joyfully to himself because he thinks he can now be a boy for ever; and he fears that if they catch him they will compel him to grow into a man, so he runs farther from them into the wood and is running still, singing to himself because he is always to be a boy.'

Peter Pan holds a peculiar position: his is the only story of recent centuries to escape from literature into folklore. For every one person who has seen the play or read the story there are hundreds who know perfectly well who and what Peter Pan is. Besides being a fairy-tale character, he is also a symbol—of what, precisely, even Barrie could not find words to describe: 'I'm youth, I'm joy! I'm a little bird that has broken out of the egg!' cries Peter—and Hook cannot understand, but says blankly, 'Oh. . . . Well, to it again,' as he raises his cutlass.

Peter Pan was created in Kensington Gardens, in the course of stories told to a party of small boys day after day and week after week: but how he began neither Barrie nor any of them could ever remember. 'I made Peter by rubbing the five of you violently together, as savages with two sticks produce a flame.'

34

The boys were the children of Arthur Llewelyn Davies and Sylvia, the daughter of George du Maurier and sister of Gerald, who played Captain Hook and many other leads in Barrie's plays. Barrie, with his big dog Porthos, met them in the Gardens and told stories that began with the old fairy tales and wandered away, in and out of legend and literature, introducing himself, Porthos, the boys and occasionally other young friends. From four years of story-telling grew his oddest book, the jumble of whimsy, magic and delight called *The Little White Bird* (1902), six chapters of which were afterwards extracted and accompanied by the finest of all Arthur Rackham's illustrations under the title of *Peter Pan in Kensington Gardens* (1906).

For anyone brought up on this book Kensington Gardens has become an extra province of Fairyland. It is hard to believe that the bird sanctuary in the Serpentine was ever known as anything but Peter Pan's Island, and in 1954 *The Times* recognised his ownership in an article on the restoration of the chains intended to keep all human visitors from its shores:

'This is the island on which Peter Pan used to land in his nightly adventures, and perhaps he still does so; but the Ministry of Works have not extended the privilege to anyone else.'

These adventures of Peter Pan precede those in the Never, Never Land: 'I ran away the day I was born,' he tells Wendy. 'I want always to be a little boy and to have fun. So I ran away to Kensington Gardens and lived a long, long time among the fairies.' *The Little White Bird* was for adults, and writing rather quizzically of the little boy David for whom the stories are supposed to be told, Barrie develops the small child's myth that babies were birds before being sent to their mothers. For this reason Peter Pan is a baby whom his mother forgets to weigh, so that he can still fly. When running, or rather flying, away he naturally returns to the island in the Serpentine from which he came, and is marooned there as soon as he realises he is not a bird: with loss of faith he loses the power of flight. The birds build the Thrush's Nest for him to sail to the Gardens, and he becomes the Fairies' playfellow, his main adventure being when he meets the little girl Maimie, who hides after the gates are shut with the object of seeing him. It is for her that the first Wendy House is built by the fairies, when she falls asleep in the snow; and it is because he is still only a baby that Peter Pan, who knows no better, holds out his hand for a kiss and puts up his face for a thimble.

At the end of *The Little White Bird* the narrator retains David's allegiance by moving on from fairy tales to stories of 'wrecked islands'; and this exactly parallels the growth of the legend—and of the Davies boys. For in 1901 they came to stay near Tilford in Surrey, only a little way from the house on the shore of the Black Lake which the Barries had bought the previous summer.

The stories were resumed, but were now concerned with pirates, redskins and desert islands; there were games besides stories, and Barrie took numerous photographs of the three elder boys—'We set out to be wrecked'—with Porthos in attendance, sometimes masquerading as a tiger. An old suit and a black mask roughly stuffed with bracken served for 'the pirate Swarthy', to be strung up in the final moment of triumph.

After the holiday Barrie prepared a book to celebrate it, of which only two copies were printed, called *The Boy Castaways of Black Lake Island*, bound to resemble the early editions of *Treasure Island* and consisting of a Preface and List of Chapters parodying such stories as *The Swiss Family Robinson* and *The Coral Island*; but instead of text there are only the thirty-six photographs, each with a suitable caption.

A chance visit to the theatre with the Davies boys to see Seymour Hicks and Ellaline Terriss (who had played Valentine Brown and Phoebe Throssel) in their own children's entertainment, *Bluebell in Fairyland*, at Christmas 1901 turned Barrie's thoughts towards writing a play for children himself. With *The Little White Bird* off his hands at the end of the summer of 1902, he began revolving ideas and making notes: 'What children like best is imitation of real boys and girls (not so much *comic* business),' which pointed out the weakness in *Bluebell*. Then came an actual line spoken by Peter Davies, 'Mother, how did we get to know you?', and the sudden recollection of Tommy Sandys's story: 'Play: "The Happy Boy": boy who couldn't grow up—runs away from pain and death—is caught *wild*. . . .'

The Boy was obviously Peter Pan; the children would be modelled on those boys whom he knew most intimately, George and John and Peter and Michael and Nicholas. . . . Then *The Boy Castaways* fell into place, Peter Pan grew to their age but was never to grow any older, and the outlines of the play began to unfold themselves before him.

There must be a heroine, a younger and more innocent Grizel whom Peter Pan could only think of as his mother —and an early child friend, W. E. Henley's little daughter, Margaret, stepped into place. She had made a very special impression on Barrie before her tragic death at the age of five—'one might call it a sudden idea that came to her in the middle of her romping'—and he had already enshrined her as the child Reddy in the early chapters of *Sentimental Tommy*. But now she was to find her place in folklore, with a name that had never been heard before: 'You my fwendy—I your little "wendy",' she had said to Barrie, and a new name was born.

Now the story was growing; Barrie insisted that what he used was only a fraction of what was there, but he alone could draw out the very essence of childhood and the imaginative world into which most children can retire. Perhaps it was because he himself could still slip away—escape, if you like—for brief moments into that world. Unlike Tommy, he could still find the golden ladder into it, even if, in the world of everyday, some penalty must be demanded of him as the price of readmission.

Fairy tale and adventure story, legend and history, yielded scraps of coloured glass that would fall into place in the kaleidoscope of his mind to form the picture that was to be *Peter Pan*. Real chronicles of the buccaneers, besides *Treasure Island* and the 'penny dreadfuls' of his schooldays, yielded up the pirates; *Peter Schlemihl* the detachable shadow; 'wrecked islands' innumerable loomed above the horizon from Crusoe to Crichton; Good Dog Tray sat down to Frederick's dinner in *Struwwelpeter*—but Porthos had actually assumed the shape of William Paterson in *The Little White Bird*. Maimie's fairy dwelling was ready to be built as soon as Wendy should sing:

> 'I wish I had a darling house,
>   The littlest ever seen,
> With funny little red walls
>   And roof of mossy green.

while the children who fell out of their perambulators were ready to grow into Lost Boys and become Peter's followers in the Never, Never Land—a name which detached itself automatically from a real district in Australia to become the one and only island of eternal make-believe.

But the essentials were all the old dreams of children and storytellers since the world began: to fly, to run away from the responsibilities of growing up and yet to assume all the prerogatives of the grown-up, to fight without being hurt, to kill without shedding blood or causing pain, to flirt with death the unrealised—'To die will be an awfully big adventure!' 'I thought it was only flowers that died. . . . Perhaps she's frightened of being dead'—and, drawing nearer to the particular, to build a hut, to live in a cave, to foil pirates and redskins, mermaids and wolves, to sail a ship, to be marooned. . . . We have all been to our own Never, Never Land and known its possibilities. This 'map of a child's mind,' wrote Barrie, 'is always more or less an island, with astonishing splashes of colour here and there, and coral reefs and rakish-looking craft in the offing, and savages and lonely lairs, and gnomes who are mostly tailors, and caves through which a river runs, and princes with six elder brothers, and a hut fast going to decay. . . .' The island has always room for more details: a corner of Tarzan's jungle or a back entrance to Kôr, a scrap of lunar landscape or a province of Narnia. But in its essentials it is still the same and ever present, though Barrie alone of mortals caught it for a magic moment and brought away a reflection of it that nearly all of us can recognise.

Denis Mackail wrote of *Peter Pan*:

'Though he put his heart and soul and all his thoughts into it, something deeper and still more individual had actually guided his pen. An alchemy, as mysterious and often as disturbing to him as to anyone else, which had taken his own sadness and nostalgia for childhood, his games with the little Davieses, and thirty years of constant if not always conscious preoccupation with the stage, and had turned them into dialogue and direction, and three hours of magic, utterly different from anything yet known.'

The penalty of a great work of art is that as soon as it is written or acted everyone can say how obvious and inevitable, and even easy, it is: in other words, that the author has captured a corner of the universal experience which no one had set to words or music or canvas

40

before. Thus it is difficult to realise how utterly new, original and different *Peter Pan* was when Barrie was ready to look for a manager in 1904.

The play, he knew, would be a complete gamble and yet demand many and costly settings, besides a company of about fifty. So, acting on the principle concerning which he punned later in *Rosy Rapture*: 'All Gaul is divided into Tree parts', he began by reading it to Beerbohm Tree, already famous for his fabulous productions at His Majesty's Theatre. But Tree was not amused, and even went so far as to warn Barrie's usual manager, the American impresario Charles Frohman, that this remarkable author had gone out of his mind.

But Frohman was so thrilled with *Peter Pan* that he set to work on it at once, sparing no expense, and introduced it to the world at the Duke of York's Theatre, London, on December 27th, 1904, with five elaborate sets and two front-drops, with costumes by William Nicholson (but the first Peter Pan collar by Henry J. Ford, illustrator of the Andrew Lang Fairy Books) and with Nina Boucicault, Gerald du Maurier, Hilda Trevelyan and George Shelton as, it is generally agreed, the best Peter, Hook, Wendy and Smee in all the play's astonishing stage history.

The first night was packed, with a mainly adult audience, but the orchestra had no need to lead the clapping to save Tinker Bell's life; the critics (except Max Beerbohm) were laudatory, but there were, it is said, a few days of uncertainty. Then the play exerted its spell and drew young and old to pack its houses with enthusiasts, as it has continued to do from that day to this in more than twelve thousand performances in Great Britain alone. Perhaps fifteen million of us have seen *Peter Pan* during the last fifty-six years. It was as popular in America, Maude Adams as Peter touring for long periods besides reviving it several times in New York, where there have been several major productions of recent years, besides a number of seasons by Eva le Gallienne in the late 'twenties and early 'thirties. It has been translated and produced with success in France, Italy and Germany—and doubtless in many other countries too, both English-speaking and otherwise, of which no records are available.

The original production was by Dion Boucicault, brother of the first Peter Pan, and when the first run ended on April 1st, 1905, it was announced that it would be resumed on December 19th. Boucicault was in charge for many years, and was succeeded by his stage-manager Lichfield Owen, who in time handed on to Cecil King the same, original production, which only ended in 1954 after half a century. As clothes, props or scenery wore out, they were replaced by exact reproductions; some of the garments survived to the end, and Hook's original coat became an heirloom worn at least once by every one of Gerald du Maurier's successors.

Even the cast never changed completely. George Shelton, the original Smee, played the part for twenty-four years, while James English and John Kelt as Jukes and Noodler scored twenty-eight—only to be surpassed by William Luff, present holder of the record, with forty-five years between 1906 and 1953. 'I never want to see *Peter Pan* without Luff as Cecco,' said Barrie, and he can seldom have done so—with the notable exception of the 1927-8 revival, when Luff played Captain Hook throughout the London run, a part which, as official understudy, he played for short periods on many other occasions, and several times in the early tours.

As Hook, William Luff was surpassed by Lionel Gadsden, who played it for seventeen long tours (over 2,500 performances) in the period between 1913 and 1938, when a duplicate company opened in the provinces before Christmas and toured for an average of four months. For nearly all of us who saw *Peter Pan* outside London before 1935 Lionel Gadsden was the one and only Captain Hook. In his old age he returned to the play, twice as Great Big Little Panther, and every year since 1955 as Noodler: at the age of eighty he was still able to give a fine performance as Hook when the principal fell ill.

These are only a few of the records: for example Peter Cotes has at various times played John, Slightly and Starkey; Jane Baxter has been a Redskin, Mrs Darling and Peter Pan, and so on. The most famous Peters have been Pauline Chase who played it for eight revivals and Jean Forbes-Robertson who played it for nine, but the list includes a galaxy of stars ranging from Fay Compton and Gladys Cooper to Ann Todd and Margaret Lockwood, just as, after du Maurier, we may select the most notable Hooks from Henry Ainley, Ralph Richardson, Alastair Sim, Charles Laughton and Donald Wolfit. Hilda Trevelyan has never been surpassed: 'You are Wendy and there will never be another to touch you,' wrote Barrie in 1920, and she played the part for nine seasons: those who saw her and have seen most of her successors award the second place to Joyce Redman. Only four actresses seem to have played both Wendy and Peter: Lila Maravan, Dinah Sheridan, Joan Greenwood and Julia Lockwood.

The only name that has never changed on any *Peter Pan* programme is that of Jane Wren (sometimes Jenny in the provinces) as Tinker Bell, even during the one season (1911) when a real actress, Anna Langley, played the part behind a 'minimising' glass. For Miss Wren (although she once received a demand note from H.M. Inspector of Taxes) is only the reflection of a spotlight from a tiny mirror in the stage-manager's hand, and her voice is a collar of bells and two special ones (to say 'You silly ass!') which Barrie brought from Switzerland.

The Peter Pan legend is not confined to the play. He did not only fly straight across the footlights and out into folk-lore and have his name taken in vain by innumerable makers of toys or clothes for the young. On May 1st, 1912, his statue by Sir George Frampton appeared suddenly in Kensington Gardens, on the bank of the Serpentine where he first landed from the Thrush's Nest; and, more formally, Pauline Chase unveiled a replica in Liverpool in 1928.

She had already edited *Peter Pan's Postbag*, consisting of letters from children sent to Peter Pan himself at the Duke of York's Theatre, in 1909; and Wendy or Smee could boast almost as big a fan-mail. But Peter Pan was already being re-told in story form (notably by Daniel O'Connor and Mary Byron), and there were soon *The Peter Pan Alphabet—Painting Book—Keepsake*, and so on. In fact there are so many versions and variants of *Peter Pan* that Frank Eyre wrote in his *Twentieth Century Children's Books* in 1952 that,

'. . . only a portion of the children who read it do so in Barrie's own words, but the tale itself is such an inspired amalgam of a dozen familiar and inspired ingredients that it survives all adaptation. It may very well in the end be more likely to live as a traditional nursery story, told in innumerable versions, like *Cinderella* or *Little Red Riding Hood*, than as an individual piece of creative writing.'

The play was not published until 1928, when Barrie revised it considerably, and wrote many delightful stage directions, besides an amusing Introduction, the 'Dedication' to the Davies boys. However, in 1911 he had made the play into a book, *Peter and Wendy* (*Peter Pan and Wendy* in later editions); so good a book that it is surprising to find the short versions still being re-issued. It is even stranger to find how comparatively little known the real book seems to be.

The style is not always easy for the child reader, and a few of the conceits are definitely of the adult Barrie variety; but these are only stray motes in the sunbeam. All the play is digested into the story, and much more besides, with a finality and a conviction that only Barrie could achieve. All the questions are answered, too, including what happened 'When Wendy Grew Up', which Barrie wrote first as an additional scene to the play, *An Afterthought*, which was acted for a single performance (February 22nd, 1908) and published for the first time in its original form in 1957. Altogether *Peter Pan and Wendy* is a perfect book for children, and children who find it at the right age are engrossed by it and remember it vividly. It should be better known, and would gain by appearing in some popular edition, and certainly with worthy illustrations: in this respect it has never been well served.

Barrie wrote another version of *Peter Pan* which is the least known of any: a scenario for a silent film that was never made. This waif of the Never, Never Land, which was first published in 1954 in the present author's *Fifty Years of 'Peter Pan'*, can stand comparison unflinchingly with Peter Pan's other two media, and contains many delightful touches and intriguing suggestions not to be found in either but every bit as genuine and authentic.

Though Barrie's scenario was not used, a silent film of *Peter Pan* appeared in 1924, little more than an uninspired imitation of the play. Walt Disney turned the story into a coloured cartoon film in 1953 and achieved a much more worthy result, proving in his own way that the legend can stand on its own without much help from Barrie, though only as a thrilling game with the deeper magic in abeyance.

Meanwhile the play is still revived each Christmas and continues to pack houses twice daily for five weeks in London and ten in the provinces. In 1954 a completely new production was launched, with many cuts in the script so as to allow the central act, 'The Mermaid's Lagoon', to return from many years of exile. Superb sets and costumes, intelligent, and for the last few years

46

a loving, production, and a dashing sense of excitement more than compensate for what has been lost, and make of it a new revelation and a new joy. Only something of the magic is missing, since no Peter seems able to catch the eeriness of Nina Boucicault or the intangible and fey quality of Jean Forbes-Robertson, and some of the key lines have gone in consequence. Some also of the lines that evoke the underlying depth have disappeared, the shadow of tragedy in the background which for the adult theatre-goer makes *Peter Pan* something more than the best play for children ever written.

IV. Lob's Wood

Barrie, wrote the *Observer's* leader-writer the day after his death, was 'a romantic who could suddenly turn round and write the realists off the stage. It is customary nowadays to make fun of his excursions into fairyland. That he made greater excursions elsewhere is too easily forgotten.'

Although *Peter Pan* stands alone and, taken as a whole conception, is one of the few supreme contributions to children's literature,* it is not his only great work. Without it, indeed, he would probably hold at this moment a much higher place as a dramatist, or at least be taken more seriously as such. Writers of the greatest works for children seem to have become the natural prey of the psycho-analysts, and Barrie even more than Lewis Carroll or Kenneth Grahame has proved an irresistible target for their attentions. There seems to have been more excuse for their interest in his case than in either of the others, for the 'mark set on a boy's soul' by Margaret Ogilvy was never quite obliterated, and the failure of his marriage with the divorce of his wife on an adultery charge in 1909 suggests that there was something of autobiography in Grizel's quandary:

'He did not love her. "Not as I love him", she said to herself. "Not as married people ought to love, but in

---

* F. J. Harvey Darton in his *Children's Books in England* (1932), the standard work on the subject, wrote of *Peter Pan* that it 'has influenced the spirit of children's books, and the grown-up view of them, more powerfully than any other work except the *Alices* and Andersen's *Fairy Tales*'.

the other way he loves me dearly." By the other way she meant that he loved her as he loved Elspeth [his sister], and loved them both just as he had loved them when all three played in the den. He was a boy who could not grow up.'

Such handicaps, and whatever of tragedy comes from them, should be the private concern of the sufferer only; however, inevitably in the case of an author they have some effect on his work and are deemed to be of public interest. But while the psychological background may help to form a work of art, it is false logic to assume that the work of art is rendered unhealthy by any oddness in the spiritual equipment of the author. Because Barrie was endowed with an abnormal power of re-entering his childhood, it must not be thought that the childhood he depicted in his writings was therefore abnormal: it is not the past that is morbid, but the desire to escape too often into it. Whatever Barrie's own experience may have been, or however great his temptation, all that concerns us is the work of art that results. *Peter Pan* can be accepted fully by the child: it is childhood enjoyed to the full, as each age and experience should be. Barrie might just as well be accused of a 'middle-age' complex for writing his one-act play *Rosalind* (1912) in which the middle-aged actress, Beatrice Page, escapes from her artificial youthfulness in theatrical life to revel in every detail of her actual age when on holiday.

Peter Pan was always, to Barrie, 'the tragic boy', and the tragedy is plain for the adult reader or theatre-goer. But a children's play was not the play for 'writing the realists off the stage'.

Barrie took, as it were, a breathing space after *Peter Pan*, with the slight and rather artificial full-length play *Alice-Sit-by-the-Fire* (1905), two whimsical scraps of gossamer, the one-act 'toy tragedies' of *Pantaloon* (1905) and *Punch* (1906) and the topical and completely ephemeral revue sketch, *Josephine* (1906), before writing one of his most enduring plays, *What Every Woman Knows* (1908). This is realism as a fine art, quiet satire and deep understanding of humanity, dressed in all the outward charm and graciousness of which he was a master: it shares with *The Admirable Crichton* the distinction of being the most acceptable of his plays to the present prosaic age.

Little work of note appeared for some years after this. A period of depression followed the divorce in 1909, and much of his time was given up to the five sons of Arthur and Sylvia Llewelyn Davies, the child-friends of Kensington Gardens and Black Lake, whom he began to help when their father died unexpectedly in 1907, and adopted completely in 1910 on their mother's death. When troubles came, Barrie tended to shut himself away from even his closest friends, but the depression did not last, and it is a mistake to think of him as the lonely, tormented soul with a morbid bias towards pessimism, which is the impression that some of his biographers tend to leave with us.

One of his adopted sons writes:

'My memory of Barrie, if it has its portion of melancholy, is heavily tilted towards fun and incomparable sparkle. He was a man of extremes and when he was sad he was sadder than death; but so far at any rate as I was concerned, ninety per cent of the time he was an irresistible delight.'

In fact, with his intensely introspective and imaginative temperament, he was like his own Beatrice Page as Charles describes her in *Rosalind*: 'If you weren't all glee you were the saddest thing on earth.' And sad or gleeful, he was intensely generous, and ready always with help where it was most needed, and nearly always so unostentatiously that the majority of his benefactions remain unknown. Of those which could not be hidden the gift of all rights and royalties in *Peter Pan* to the Great Ormond Street Hospital for Sick Children in 1929 is the most famous. There were many others during the Great War of 1914-18, beginning with the hospital at Wrest Park (which finds a place in *A Kiss for Cinderella*) and the more famous one at Bettancourt in France, and exemplified in the sketches and playlets which he wrote for charity performances, such as *The Fatal Typist* (1915), *Shakespeare's Legacy* (1916), *Reconstructing the Crime* (1917), and *La Politesse* (1918) —trifles long forgotten, but guaranteed to bring packed houses to swell the funds of the good causes for which they were given.

After 1908 one-act plays were, for some time, all that Barrie had to offer: *Old Friends*, *The Twelve-Pound Look* (both 1910), *Rosalind* (1912), and *Half an Hour* and *The Will* in 1913. In that year the next full-length play appeared, Barrie's one complete failure, *The Adored One* (acted with a little more success in America as *The Legend of Leonora*). The brilliant first act was afterwards made into a separate 'curtain-raiser' as *Seven Women*; but the rest is rightly buried in oblivion—the only case where the whimsy of which he is so often accused is so much in evidence as to get the better of his sense of theatre.

With the outbreak of war, Barrie turned his mind to the entertainment of the troops on leave, and attempted a full-scale revue, called *Rosy Rapture*: slight but amusing, with ample scope for the chorus headed by the beautiful Gaby Deslys, round whom the trifle of plot was built, but little of the true Barrie in it.

The next real play, *A Kiss for Cinderella* (March 16th, 1916), dates a little, or has not quite become a period piece; but the central scene of Cinderella's dream, 'The Ball at the Palace' as a little London slum child would imagine it, is quite ageless, and a delightful memory for those of us who are lucky enough to have seen the play as children. There have been several revivals in London, and many by repertory companies; but it has slipped out of fashion lately, and is overdue for a return. It is not, of course, in the same class as *Peter Pan*, but high on our meagre list of children's stage classics.

The one-act plays also continued, now with some reference to the War in them, such as *Der Tag* (1914), *The New Word* (1915), *The Old Lady Shows Her Medals* (1917), and *A Well-Remembered Voice* (1918). But in 1917 Barrie felt that he had used up all his good ideas and would never write a first-class play again. He was living by now in his high flat in Adelphi Terrace overlooking the Thames, and in February of that year his friend A. E. W. Mason, on leave from the Secret Service, came to stay with him. Many years afterwards, Mason wrote:

'I have the clearest possible recollection of that episode. I was in Barrie's flat, in bed for a week with bronchitis deepening into pneumonia. During that week Barrie told me that he was worried because he could not think of any subject to work upon. I said that I remembered that before his divorce he had begun on what I thought was probably the best theme he had ever struck —that of a group of people who were always saying: "Oh! if we could begin again!" And they did begin again and did exactly as they had done the first time. Barrie had forgotten all about it. . . . He sat down to work practically at once.'

Dear Brutus ('The fault, dear Brutus, is not in our stars, but in ourselves') was finished in a few months and had its first night on October 17th, 1917, after which it ran for 365 performances and has had three successful revivals in the West End, besides innumerable touring, repertory and amateur productions. This excursion into fairyland in search of the deepest realism is held by many to be Barrie's greatest play, and is certainly the most typical and shows his genius at its highest peak. Although described as a comedy, there are undertones of tragedy as the couples slip out into Lob's Wood to have their second chance, only to make the same choice as before as they pass before us, their secret selves revealed, in the magic moonlight; yet in the last act they find the quiet and sufficient philosophy of acceptance of things as they have turned out. Only for Dearth, who has found his dream-daughter in the Wood, is there real tragedy, but for him most of all there is hope, since for the Dearths alone of the party the might-have-been is still the might-be which is 'only for the brave ones'. When all seems over, the Dearths pass across the stage outside the window hand in hand, looking not to the past but to the future. And Margaret the dream-child steals timidly across behind them.

'Barrie with a plot and Barrie expressing a philosophy on which he had mused for years', wrote Denis Mackail, 'and, in its own mood and convention, as near as almost nothing to a flawless play.'

He could not quite repeat his success, though *Mary Rose* (April 22nd, 1920) had an even more overwhelming reception, ran longer, had books written about it and was twice revived within its first ten years. But the story, based on the old Scottish legends or folk-tales of mortals who have disappeared into fairyland for many years and returned not a day older and with no memory of the missing years, lacks the underlying philosophy which in *Dear Brutus* overcomes the essentially modern reaction against any mixture of realism and the marvellous. *Mary Rose* captured and held spellbound large audiences for many hundreds of performances; but we can only take their word for its absolutely magical effect as a theatrical experience, since it has not appeared on the London stage for over thirty years and would certainly need superlative acting and production to achieve its full effect.

This was Barrie's last play for sixteen years. He had

already written the first act of a murder play, so brilliantly constructed that it seemed impossible to work it out through the subsequent acts. That he would have done so is not open to doubt, but he was writing it very much at the insistence of the favourite among his adopted sons, Michael Davies who was still an undergraduate at Oxford. On May 19th, 1921, Michael was bathing in a favourite but dangerous pool at Sandford Lasher and was dragged down into the race of the weir: his friend Rupert Buxton tried to save him, but both were drowned.

Michael's death was the worst blow Barrie ever received. 'He never got over it,' says Mr Mackail. 'It altered and darkened everything for the rest of his life.' Certainly he had no heart to continue and to finish the play, but it was acted again and again as *Shall We Join the Ladies?*—one of the most perfect of curtain-raisers.

Barrie wrote little more, but during the next ten years he cultivated the art of oratory, and became celebrated as a public speaker. His best known speech, *Courage*, made when he was Lord Rector of St Andrews University, was published separately in 1922; but the posthumous volume, *M'Connachie and J.M.B.* (1938), contains many more as well worth reading.

A selection of his early articles, mainly from *The St James's Gazette*, served him for the basis of a pleasant volume of reminiscences, *The Greenwood Hat*, printed privately in 1930 and published in 1937. A short story *Neil and Tintinnabulum: An Interlude for Parents*, contributed in 1925 to *The Flying Carpet*, a collection of children's stories edited by his secretary Lady Cynthia Asquith, showed little of the old inspiration. But in 1931 appeared *Farewell, Miss Julie Logan*, a long short story harking back suddenly to the neighbourhood of Kirriemuir, but with all the skill of construction and compression that he had lacked in the days of the Thrums novels: perfect of its kind, full of wistful charm, and a worthy pendant to his life's work.

Then suddenly in 1934 a chance suggestion from a new star actress, Elisabeth Bergner, set Barrie writing his last and most unexpected play. *The Boy David* was neither like anything he had written, nor like anything that was being written. Its production was accompanied by an almost sensational run of bad luck, and it finally reached London at a time when all thoughts were fixed on the abdication of King Edward VIII, was put on in far too big a theatre and in too lavish a style, and lacked Barrie's presence, owing to illness, at the final rehearsals and the trial run to packed houses in Edinburgh.

'A marvellous piece of philosophic and mystic thinking and creation,' wrote Rosaline Masson after the first night. 'I don't think "Shakespearean" is an exaggerated term to use.' But the London critics in December 1936 thought otherwise, and the vastness of His Majesty's Theatre was only crammed when it was announced that the play was about to be withdrawn.

Yet, though the plot falters during the visions in the third act, Barrie's picture of David in the days before he became King of Israel has a stage magic and a wistful poetry entirely its own, and these come across perfectly in a small theatre and an intimate production.

Barrie was a dying man when the original production came to an end after only fifty-five performances, and the disappointment was severe. He died quietly on June 19th, 1937, aged seventy-seven, and was buried with his own people in a simple grave in the cemetery at Kirriemuir.

'When a great man dies,' wrote Barrie after the death of George Meredith, 'the immortals await him at the top of the nearest hill.' With them the author of *Dear Brutus* and *The Admirable Crichton* would be sure of his place even if he had not written *Peter Pan*. This, his most enduring creation, gives him as assured a niche near the top of another summit. On the drop curtain (painted to look like an old sampler sewn by Wendy) which he designed for *Peter Pan* he wrote, 'Dear Hans Christian Andersen. Dear Charles Lamb. Dear Lewis Carroll. Dear Robert Louis Stevenson.' We may without hesitation add, 'Dear J. M. Barrie.'

A BARRIE BOOK LIST

II. PLAYS
(other than revue sketches and ephemera)

[One-act plays are indicated by an asterisk *. Final date is of first publication; where none is given, the play remains unpublished. Those followed by the letter [C] are included in *The Definitive Edition of the Plays of J. M. Barrie*, 1942. The plays were published by Hodder and Stoughton, except where other publishers are given].

*Caught Napping. [Never acted]. 1883. [Privately Printed].

Richard Savage [with H. B. Marriott Watson]. (Criterion, April 16th, 1891). 1891. [Privately Printed].

*Ibsen's Ghost. (Toole's Theatre, May 30th, 1891).

Walker, London. (Toole's Theatre, February 25th, 1892). Samuel French, 1907. [C].

Jane Annie, or The Good Conduct Prize. [Libretto in collaboration with A. Conan Doyle]. (Savoy, May 13th, 1893). Chappell, 1893.

The Professor's Love Story. (Star [New York], December 19th, 1892; Comedy [London], June 26th, 1894). [C].

The Little Minister (Haymarket, November 6th, 1897). [C].

The Wedding Guest. (Garrick, September 27th, 1900). Fortnightly Review, 1900. [C].

Quality Street. (Vaudeville, September 17th, 1902). 1913. [C].

The Admirable Crichton. (Duke of York's, November 4th, 1902). 1914. [C].

Little Mary. (Wyndham's, September 24th, 1903). [C].

Peter Pan. (Duke of York's, December 27th, 1904). 1928. [C].

*Pantaloon. (Duke of York's, April 5th, 1905). 1914. [C].

Alice-Sit-by-the-Fire. (Duke of York's, April 5th, 1905). 1919. [C].

*Punch. (Comedy, April 5th, 1906).

*When Wendy Grew Up: An Afterthought. (Duke of York's, February 22nd, 1908). Nelson, 1957.

What Every Woman Knows. (Duke of York's, September 3rd, 1908). 1918. [C].

*Old Friends. (Duke of York's, March 1st, 1910). 1928. [C].

*The Twelve-Pound Look. (Duke of York's, March 1st, 1910). 1914. [C].

*A Slice of Life. (Duke of York's, June 7th, 1910).

*Rosalind. (Duke of York's, October 14th, 1912). 1914. [C].

*The Will. (Duke of York's, September 4th, 1913). 1914. [C].

The Adored One. (Duke of York's, September 4th, 1913). [Revised as The Legend of Leonora, Empire, New York, January 5th, 1914].

*Half an Hour. (Hippodrome, September 29th, 1913). 1928. [C].

*Der Tag. (Coliseum, December 21st, 1914). 1914.

*The New Word. (Duke of York's, March 22nd, 1915). 1918. [C].

Rosy Rapture. [Revue]. (Duke of York's, March 22nd, 1915).

A Kiss for Cinderella. (Wyndham's, March 16th, 1916). 1920.

*Seven Women. (New, April 7th, 1917). 1928. [C].

*The Old Lady Shows Her Medals. (New, April 7th, 1917). 1918. [C].

Dear Brutus. (Wyndham's, October 17th, 1917). 1923. [C].

*A Well-Remembered Voice. (Wyndham's, June 28th, 1918). 1918. [C].

*Barbara's Wedding. (Savoy, August 23rd, 1927). 1918. [C].

*The Truth About the Russian Dancers. (Coliseum, March 16th, 1920).

Mary Rose. (Haymarket, April 22nd, 1920). 1924. [C].

*Shall We Join the Ladies? (R.A.D.A., May 27th, 1921). 1927. [C].

The Boy David. (His Majesty's, November 21st, 1936). Peter Davies, 1938. [C].

———

*The Fight for Mr Lapraik. [Written 1917. No professiona production]. 1947 (in *New Plays Quarterly*).

Scenario for a Silent Film of 'Peter Pan'. [Written 1920. Not used. First published in Roger Lancelyn Green's *Fifty Years of 'Peter Pan'*, Peter Davies, 1954].

———

Half Hours, published 1914, contained *Pantaloon, The Twelve-Pound Look, Rosalind,* and *The Will.*

Echoes of the War, published 1918, contained *The Old Lady Shows Her Medals, The New Word, Barbara's Wedding* and *A Well-Remembered Voice.*

Shall We Join the Ladies? and Other Plays, published 1928, also contained *Half an Hour, Seven Women* and *Old Friends.*

The Definitive Edition of the Plays of J. M. Barrie in one volume [plays marked [C] in list above] was published by Hodder and Stoughton in 1942. (The first Collected Edition in 1928 contained six fewer full-length plays).

———

III. MISCELLANEOUS WRITINGS

A. Pamphlets and Speeches.
Allahakbarries C.C. [Privately printed]. 1893.
Scotland's Lament: A Poem on the Death of R. L. Stevenson. (*The Bookman*, January 1895, and as privately printed pamphlet). 1895.
The Allahakbarrie Book of Broadway Cricket. [Privately printed]. 1899. Published (as *Allahakbarries C.C. 1899*). James Barrie, 1950.
George Meredith. Constable, 1909.
Charles Frohman: A Tribute. (*Daily Mail*, May 10th, and privately printed pamphlet).
Courage. [Speech at St Andrews, May 3rd, 1922]. Hodder and Stoughton, 1922.
The Entrancing Life. [Speech at Edinburgh, October 25th, 1930]. Hodder and Stoughton, 1930.

B. Contributions to Books by other writers include
Preface to R. M. Ballantyne's *The Coral Island.* James Nisbet, 1913.
Introduction to Charles Turley's *The Voyages of Captain Scott.* Smith, Elder, 1914.
Preface to Daisy Ashford's *The Young Visiters.* Chatto and Windus, 1919.
'Neil and Tintinnabulum'. *The Flying Carpet.* Edited by Cynthia Asquith. Partridge, 1925.
'The Blot on Peter Pan'. *The Treasure Ship.* Edited by Cynthia Asquith. Partridge, 1926.

C. Theatrical Miscellanea. All unpublished
Becky Sharp. [One-act adaptation from *Vanity Fair*]. (Terry's Theatre, June 3rd, 1893).
A Platonic Friendship. [Duologue]. (Drury Lane, March 17th, 1898).
Josephine. [Revue in three scenes]. (Comedy, April 5th, 1906).
The Dramatists Get What They Wanted. [One-act burlesque]. (Hippodrome, December 23rd, 1912).
The Ladies' Shakespeare. [One-act burlesque]. (Hamilton, Ont., Canada, October 26th, 1914).

The Fatal Typist. [Playlet for charity]. (His Majesty's, November 19th, 1915).

The Real Thing At Last. [Short burlesque film]. (Coliseum, February 7th, 1916).

Shakespeare's Legacy. [Playlet for charity]. (Drury Lane, April 14th, 1916). [Privately printed 1916].

Reconstructing the Crime. [Entertainment for charity]. (Palace, February 16th, 1917).

The Origin of Harlequin. [Ballet]. (Palace, February 16th, 1917; Wyndhams, June 28th 1918).

La Politesse. [Playlet for charity]. (Wyndhams, June 28th, 1918).

D. *Private Entertainments* (*usually acted for or by children*). *All unpublished*

Bandelero the Bandit. (Dumfries Amateur Dramatic Club, 1877).

The Greedy Dwarf. (133 Gloucester Road, January 7th, 1901).

The Cinema Supper. (Scala Theatre, July 3rd, 1914).

Where Was Simon? (Stanway, Gloucestershire: January 16th, 1926).

The Wheel: A Play for Eight Children and their Grandpapa. (Stanway, April 18th, 1927).

IV. BOOKS ABOUT J. M. BARRIE

J. M. Barrie and His Books: Biographical and Critical Studies by J. A. Hammerton. Horace Marshall, 1900.

J. M. Barrie and the Theatre by H. M. Walbrook. F. V. White & Co., 1922.

J. M. Barrie: A Study in Fairies and Mortals by Patrick Braybrooke. Drane's, 1924.

A New Approach to an Analysis of 'Mary Rose' by P. L. Geitein, 1926.

Barrie by Thomas Moult. Jonathan Cape, 1928.

A Bibliography of the Writings of Sir James Matthew Barrie, Bart, O.M., by Herbert Garland. Bookman's Journal, 1928.

Barrie: The Story of a Genius by J. A. Hammerton. Sampson, Low, 1929.

J. M. Barrie by F. J. Harvey Darton. Nisbet, 1929.

Sir James Barrie als Dramatiker by W. Eschenauer. 1930.

Thrums and the Barrie Country by John Kennedy. Heath Cranton, 1930.

Sir James M. Barrie: A Bibliography by B. D. Cutler [New York], 1931.

Sir J. M. Barrie: His First Editions by Andrew Block. Foyle, 1933.

James Matthew Barrie: an Appreciation by James A. Roy. Jarrolds, 1937.

The Barrie Inspiration by Patrick Chalmers. Peter Davies, 1938.

J. M. Barrie by W. A. Darlington. Blackie, 1938.

The Story of J.M.B.: A Biography by Denis Mackail. Peter Davies, 1941.

Barrie and the Kailyard School by George Blake. Arthur Barker, 1951.

Fifty Years of 'Peter Pan' by Roger Lancelyn Green. Peter Davies, 1954.

Portrait of Barrie by Cynthia Asquith. James Barrie, 1954.

A List of Barrie's Books published in the United States

I. BOOKS
(other than plays)

Better Dead. Rand McNally, 1891.
Auld Licht Idylls. Macmillan, 1891.
When a Man's Single. Harper, 1889.
A Window in Thrums. Cassell, 1892.
My Lady Nicotine. Rand McNally, 1891.
The Little Minister. Lovell, 1891.
A Tillyloss Scandal. Lovell, 1893.
Margaret Ogilvy. Scribner, 1896.
Sentimental Tommy. Scribner, 1896.
Tommy and Grizel. Scribner, 1900.
The Little White Bird. Scribner, 1902.
Peter Pan in Kensington Gardens. Scribner, 1906.
Peter and Wendy. Scribner, 1911.
Farewell, Miss Julie Logan. Scribner, 1932.
The Greenwood Hat. Scribner, 1938.
M'Connachie and J.M.B.: Speeches by J. M. Barrie. Scribner, 1939.

2. PLAYS

Plays marked by an asterisk * are included in *The Collected Edition of the Plays of J. M. Barrie*. (See below.)

Walker, London. Samuel French, 1907.
Jane Annie, or The Good Conduct Prize. Novello, Ewer, 1893.
The Wedding Guest. Scribner, 1900.
**Quality Street.* Scribner, 1918.
The Admirable Crichton. Scribner, 1918.
**Peter Pan.* Silver Burdett, 1914.
**Pantaloon.* Hodder, 1914.
**Alice-Sit-by-the-Fire.* Scribner, 1919.
**What Every Woman Knows.* Scribner, 1915.
**The Twelve-Pound Look.* Scribner, 1914.
**Rosalind.* Scribner, 1914.
**The Will.* Scribner, 1914.
The Legend of Leonora. Rosenfield, 1913.
**Half an Hour.* Scribner, 1929.
Der Tag. Scribner, 1914.
The New Word. Scribner, 1918.
**A Kiss for Cinderella.* Scribner, 1921.
**Seven Women.* Scribner, 1929.
The Old Lady Shows Her Medals. Scribner, 1918.
**Dear Brutus.* Scribner, 1922.
Barbara's Wedding. Scribner, 1918.
**Mary Rose.* Scribner, 1924.
Shall We Join the Ladies? Scribner, 1929.
The Boy David. Scribner, 1938.

———

Half Hours, published 1914 by Scribner, contained *Pantaloon, The Twelve-Pound Look, Rosalind,* and *The Will.*

Echoes of the War, published 1918 by Scribner, contained *The Old Lady Shows Her Medals, The New Word, Barbara's Wedding* and *A Well-Remembered Voice.*

The Collected Edition of the Plays of J. M. Barrie, published 1929 by Scribner, contained plays indicated above by an asterisk*.